ERRANCES

By the same author:

Poetry
Otopos (2024)
Volte Face (2024).
Pistes de Rêve (2024).
Endgame with No Ending (2023).
After Cage: A Serial Composition in Word and Movement on Time and Silence (2022).
Kaosmos (2020).
Tracks: Autofictional Fragments of a Journey without Maps (2020).
Kosmogonies (2019).
After Cage (2019).
Crypto (with Béatrice Machet, 2018).
Hors Limites (2018).
Hush: A Fugue (2017).
Stretchmarks of Sun (2014).
Out of Bounds (2009).
Couchgrass (2006).
Good Grief: and Other Frivolous Journeys into Spells, Songs and Elegies (2002).
The Gaze of Silence (1999).

Fiction
Smacked and Other Stories of Addiction (2022).
Speculate: A Collection of Microlit (with Eugen Bacon, 2021).
Noisy Blood: Stories (2004).
The Book of Elsa: A Novel (2000).
Magic and Other Stories (2000).
Mythfits: Four Uneasy Pieces (1999).

Essays
Threading Through (2021).
Creative Writing with Critical Theory: Inhabitation (with Julian Novitz, 2018).
Towards a Poetics of Creative Writing (2015).
The Creativity Market: Creative Writing in the 21st Century (2012).
Female Sexuality: The Early Psychoanalytic Controversies (with Russell Grigg and Craig Smith, 1999).

ERRANCES

DOMINIQUE HECQ

Errances
Recent Work Press
Canberra, Australia

Copyright © Dominique Hecq, 2026

ISBN: 9781764106863 (paperback)

 A catalogue record for this book is available from the National Library of Australia

All rights reserved. This book is copyright. Except for private study, research, criticism or reviews as permitted under the Copyright Act, no part of this book may be reproduced, stored in a retrieval system, or transmitted in any form by any means without prior written permission. Enquiries should be addressed to the publisher.

Cover design: Recent Work Press
Set by Recent Work Press

recentworkpress.com

For Michael Plastow

Contents

Paso doble	1
Rondo	3
Estèné	4
Fête au village	5
Village revelry	5
Other	6
Passing through	7
On the edge of alien shores	8
In an Aussie garden	9
Metaphilosophy	10
Lull	11
Cri et silence	12
Homework	13
Unspeakable language	14
Hors-lieu	16
We live in motion	17
Coda *oi oi oi*	*18*

*Partir c'est
escalader son désarroi
sur la corde
de l'oubli*

—Samira Negrouche

Paso doble

Deux mots me viennent à l'esprit : l'anglais *lull* (accalmie) et l'espagnol *luz* (lumière).

Two words come to mind: the English word *lull* and the Spanish word *luz* (light).

J'ai rencontré le substantif *lull* dans une nouvelle de George Orwell, 'Shooting an Elephant', une violente critique du colonialisme à Burma. Le mot n'avait selon moi aucun sens dans ce récit terrible. Voyez l'étymologie : Du moyen anglais *lullen, lollen*. À l'origine, peut-être expressif des sons *la-la-la* ou *lu-lu-lu* émis pour calmer un enfant comparable au finnois *laulaa* (chanter) et à l'hiligaynon *lala* (chanter une berceuse).

I came across the noun *lull* in a short story by George Orwell, 'Shooting an Elephant', a violent critique of colonialism in Burma. The word made no sense to me in this terrible story. Consider the etymology: From Middle English *lullen, lollen*. Originally, perhaps expressive of the sounds *la-la-la* or *lu-lu-lu* made to calm a child, comparable to the Finnish *laulaa* (to sing) and the Galician *lala* (to sing a lullaby).

La *luz* me transporte toujours aux vacances de mon enfance à la Costa Brava. Le mot fusait dans l'air et ponctuait les routes : *punta de la luz, villa de la luz, hotel de la luz, playa de la luz*, etc.

Luz always transports me back to my childhood vacations on the Costa Brava. The word was everywhere, punctuating the roads: punta de la luz, villa de la luz, hotel de la luz, playa de la luz, etc.

Je note que ces deux mots commencent par la lettre L, qui nous renvoie au *la-la-la* de la petite enfance et, clin d'œil, à *lalangue* de Jacques Lacan.

I note that these two words begin with the letter L, which brings us back to the la-la-la of early childhood and, with a wink, to Jacques Lacan's *lalangue*.

Rondo

Lulled by the night's lingering breath, the city
hibernates. Sucking wind at your face, you skirt
the creek. Follow the trickle of bruises the light leaves
in its wake. You take the path down to
the bridge, the no-sun enfolded in fog.

Arrullada por el difuso aliento nocturno, la ciudad
hiberna. Aspirando el viento en la cara, bordeas
el arroyo. Sigue el reguero de magulladuras que la luz
deja a su paso. Tomas el camino que baja hacia
el puente, el no-sol envuelto en la niebla.

Bercée par le souffle de la nuit, la ville
hiberne. Le vent dans le dos, tu longes
le ruisseau. Suis le filet de bleus que la lumière
laisse dans son sillage. Tu prends le sentier qui dévale
au pont, au non-soleil enveloppé de brouillard.

Estèné

Un mot que j'affectionne particulièrement me vient du wallon liégeois. Il s'agit de l'adjectif *estèné,* qui désigne l'état confus de qui vient de recevoir un choc et qui, à mon oreille, se prête à un jeu de mot littéral esté né/est né. Je le fais danser sur les pavés, arrosé de pèquêt—un alcool blanc du terroir.

A word that I particularly like comes from the Walloon dialect of Liège. It is the adjective estèné, which describes the confused state of someone who has just received a shock and which, to my ear, lends itself to a literal play on words: esté né/est né (born/was born). I make it dance on the cobblestones, sprinkled with pèquêt—a local white liquor.

Fête au village

Le temps tournoie derrière le soleil. Bondit
dadais danseur *estèné*. *S'trèboule so l'pavèye*,
s'tape à rire comme un gosse *avou l'pèquêt*.

Village revelry

Time whirls behind the sun. Leaps
dancing *estèné*. *S'trèboule so l'pavèye*,
falls about and hoots like a kid *avou l'pèquêt*.

Other

En tant qu'étrangère en terre australe, je hais le mot *migration* [maɪˈgreɪʃən] qui désigne *the act of people moving from one place to an other* et qui signifie assimilation et intégration. Le mot migre bien : *migrazione, migración,* αποδημία, *migracija, migrace, migratie, migracja,* міграція… ou moins bien : *sự di trú en, göç,* ‌هِجْرَة. Dans ce cas, *migration* [maɪˈgreɪʃən] fait écho à *vacation* qui lui-même fait taire poliment *expulsion*.

As a foreigner in the southern hemisphere, I hate the word migration [maɪˈgreɪʃən], which refers to *the act of people moving from one place to another* and implies assimilation and integration. The word migrates well: *migrazione, migración,* αποδημία, *migracija, migrace, migratie, migracja,* міграція… or less well: *sự di trú en, göç,* ‌هِجْرَة. In this case, migration [maɪˈgreɪʃən] echoes *vacation*, which itself politely silences *expulsion*.

Passing through

Wherever you come from
or are—
with no margins

uprooted or not
you only ever write to prove that you exist.

In doing so, you lose yourself

empty yourself

dispossess yourself

destroy yourself

re-craft yourself.

Only nothingness signifies everything.

It is from loss that you draw your strength.

You pulled at your moorings
moved on
transgressed.

All the while knowing that one never leaves.

Yours is a borderline, insular, precarious, ambiguous predicament:
you keep on displacing the horizon.

On the edge of alien shores

The giant neon swan flashes
white against the black sky.

Beneath, the naked city lies on its back like Leda
knees apart in porno freeze-frame.

The freeway busts right up through.

The territory slides off the map
towards Bass Strait but you're grounded.

Decay oozes from the river. Gets into your skin.
You choke on its humid breath.

It's so hot and humid this could be Singapore or Saigon
but it's the city you now call home.

The further west you go the fewer lights
and all seems on the verge of subsidence.

Stripped out factories crumble under their weight
as mud percolates its way up through the sediment.

When the river breaks its banks the scum of petroleum
rises up the waterways, drowning the eels—*iuk iuk iuk iuk iuk.*

In an Aussie garden

The camphor laurels dividing
the houses from each other loom
and stream shadows

yours, swirls and lurches
somewhere between
nympheas and belladonnas:

your body under his scrutiny

always under his jurisdiction

on the brink of vanishing.

Metaphilosophy

Enslaved to the hypothesis of emancipation
you willingly perform in a show trial
impelled to surrender everything.

Daily humiliations remind you
the idea of universal emancipation
remains a force in the world.

The danger you face isn't oppression
but boredom posed as subjective freedom
against the hard labour of dissent.

Lull

You bask in breezy shifts that breathe life into thought

Seek spaces conducive to songs foreign to strict obedience

Uncover the hum of jingoism

Rub shoulders with outsiders whose labile ways charm you

Hanker for accommodating knowledge—the kind that breaks down compacted concrete

Choose the interjections of meanders and speckled rivers.

Cri et silence

You are made of particles in time and space, so only truly become yourself in your relationships with others. With leaps into gorges within these very relationships. At the source of all life, which is essentially the other. And which allows you to be yourself and more present to others.

You who also have a dual allegiance as human: to life and death; to time and eternity; to murder and life; to time and eternity, to the unconscious and consciousness. A dual allegiance compounded by your sex: you can give life, but also take it away.

In this world in which we live and which, in its very convulsions, is already that of tomorrow, what is required of us in the first place? If not to work towards the advent of this relationship between oneself and the other. To write.

Homework

One idea's as good as any other.

For instance, how you feel.

Out of place
Awkward
Excluded
Shitty
Diminished
Stupid
Non-existent
Culpable
Useless
Incompetent
Untrustworthy
Degraded
Dismal
Unnecessary
Fraudulent
Wrong
All over the place

Continue in this vein until you no longer… feel.

Unspeakable language

(i)

You fell in love with Spanish
learned Germanic languages

that estranged you further
from your anorectic body

(your mother was a Schumacher
with a foreclosed past)

(ii)

To return is to
climb one's distress
on the rope
of errance

(iii)

What strikes you when you come back from Spain, or France, or Belgium, for that matter, is the absence, here, among folks, of what you call gesture, not gesticulation: the expressive power, underlying speech, that is characteristic of Romance languages.

When you spy on people waiting for the tram or chatting in a café, you get the feeling that their bodies are tied up, stuffed into a casing, or like armchairs in a disused room, covered with a dusty slipcover. There is something squashed about them. Frozen. And the words that come out of their mouths are grey and dull. As if deprived of momentum and joy. Imprisoned. Disembowelled.

Words that don't rise. Fly. Soar.

Down to earth words. The opposite of the winged words Homer speaks of.

Something's missing here.

You feel ill
at ease. Cackle. Chuckle. Giggle.

Under/lying it all: anguish.

Hors-lieu

Errance qui vide qui rend sourd où le monstre vit soudain du seul alignement des mots sur la page de la mécanique des pas l'un devant l'autre dans une rue sans importance pour aller nulle part où la bouche ne parle plus de moi de toi ne demande rien ne fait plus supplique sourit dans une sorte de corps démembré qui est perdu mais sans tristesse sans la rédemption des larmes qui avance mais comme on recule qui tourne dans les phrases en vain qui ne croit en rien ne veut rien ne continue que pour les mots que pour le mot *errance* qu'on préfère au mot *oubli*.

Wandering that empties that deafens where the monster suddenly surges up from the mere alignment of words on the page from the mechanics of steps one in front of the other in some irrelevant street to go nowhere where the mouth no longer speaks of me of you asks for nothing no longer begs grins in some kind of dismembered body that is lost but with no sorrow without the redemption of tears that moves forward but as one retreats that whirls around in sentences that believes in nothing wants nothing continues only for the words only for the word *errance* that one prefers to the word *oblivion*.

We live in motion

Partir c'est
escalader son désarroi
sur la corde
de l'oubli

To leave is to
climb one's distress
on the rope
of oblivion

Coda *oi oi oi*

You watch the fog cascade over itself
like tumbleweeds under gathering clouds.

A loudspeaker blares *if we don't stop
immigration our death is certain.*

As if. Impending violence takes up residence
in your mind. Fear and tension in your body.

Notes

The poems in this chapbook were written on the unceded traditional lands of the Wurundjeri Woi Wurrung of the Kulin Nation. I acknowledge and pay my respects to their Elders, past and present, and to all the poetry spoken and sung for millennia on this Country.

The Algerian poet Samira Negrouche's poem 'Six arbres de fortune autour de ma baignoire' was reprinted in *J'habite en mouvement: Anthologie 2001-2021* (barzakh, 2023, p. 167). My sincere thanks to Samira for her generous permission to quote and translate lines from the poem.

'Rondo' is an exercise in translation. It mimics the struggle of self-translation: sometimes one can only recover one's mother tongue through resorting to a third language.

The English stanza is reproduced from the opening of *Otopos*, a work which explores the paradoxical interleaving and entangling of self and topos (Beltway Editions, 2024, p. 13).

It is as though…
lines   dodged   escaped
lines that slip between
bodies   fingers   words   tropisms   echoes
lines escaped to the margins of margins
tongues of wind   dust   light
líneas   esquivadas   escapadas
líneas que se deslizan entre
cuerpos   dedos   palabras   tropismos   ecos
líneas   escapadas al margen de los márgenes
lenguas de viento   polvo   luz.
lignes   esquivées   échappées
lignes qui glissent entre

corps   doigts   mots   tropismes   échos
lignes échappées en marge des marges
langues de vent   poussière   lumière

'On the edge of alien shores' references A. D. Hope's famous poem 'Australia'. It was first published in 1943 in the highly respected magazine *Meanjin*, though he had written it earlier.

I wish to thank Mark Ulysseas for publishing 'Passing through', 'On the edge of alien shores' and 'Cri et silence' in the online magazine *Live Encounters*.

About the author

Dominique Hecq is a widely anthologised and award-winning poet, fiction writer, essayist and translator. She lives and works on Wurundjeri Woi Wurrung land. Hecq writes in English and French. Her creative works comprise a novel, six collections of short stories and seventeen books of poetry. Together with *Volte Face* (Liquid Amber Press, Melbourne) and *Otopos* (Beltway Editions, Rockville, MD) her bilingual sequence, *Pistes de rêve* (Transignum, Paris) appeared in 2024.

Among other honours such as The Melbourne Fringe Festival Award for Outstanding Writing and Spoken Word Performance, The Woorilla Prize for Fiction, The New England Review Prize for Poetry, The Martha Richardson Medal for Poetry, and the inaugural AALITRA Prize for Literary Translation in poetry from Spanish into English, Dominique Hecq is a recipient of the 2018 International Best Poets Prize administered by the International Poetry Translation and Research Centre in conjunction with the International Academy of Arts and Letters and, more recently, the James Tate Prize for Poetry.

www.ingramcontent.com/pod-product-compliance
Lightning Source LLC
LaVergne TN
LVHW092102060526
838201LV00047B/1531